Search and Find Fairies

TOP THAT

Licensed exclusively to Top That Publishing Ltd
Tide Mill Way, Woodbridge, Suffolk, IP12 1AP, UK
www.topthatpublishing.com
Copyright © 2017 Tide Mill Media
0 2 4 6 8 9 7 5 3 1
Manufactured in China

1 pair of pretty gloves

2 garden trowels

3 flower baskets

4 toadstools

5 butterflies

The castle garden

The fairies are busy in the castle garden. Can you find all the things hidden in the pretty scene?

Can you find?

6 watering cans

7 heart-shaped trees

8 bees

9 blue birds

10 red apples

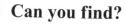

1 pink butterfly

2 blue birds

3 polishing fairies

4 arched windows

5 mopping fairies

In the magical wood

The magical wood is buzzing with fairies spring-cleaning their treehouses. How many of these things can you spot?

Can you find?

6 sweeping fairies

7 blue flowers

8 round windows

9 dusting fairies

10 brown buckets

Can you find?

1 silver fairy

2 pink fairies

3 pale purple fairies

4 red fairies

5 blue fairies

Playtime!

The fairies like nothing more than a game of hide-and-seek. Can you find the different-coloured fairies hiding amongst the flowers?

Can you find?

6 orange fairies

7 green fairies

8 dark purple fairies

9 white fairies

10 yellow fairies

Baking day

The fairies are baking and decorating fancy cakes for tea. Can you find all these things in their kitchen?

Can you find?

1 fairy cake with sprinkles

2 bowls of sprinkles

3 bags of flour

4 whisks

5 wooden spoons

6 blue
hats

7 strawberries

8 cherries

9 empty
cake cases

10 pink
hats

Can you find?

1 cake stand

2 milk jugs

3 orange slices

4 cups of juice

5 fairy cakes

Afternoon tea

It's time for afternoon tea … the fairies' favourite meal! Find all of these teatime things hidden in the scene.

6 slices
of cake

7 macarons

8 iced
buns

9 red
teacups

10 plates of
sandwiches

Can you find?

1 blue
bird

2 butterflies

3 birdcages

4 pairs of spell
books

5 wall
candles

Spell practice

Practising spells is hard work, but it's very important too!
Can you find these things hidden in the Spells Room?

Can you find?

6 candelabras

7 cobwebs

**8 bags
of fairy dust**

**9 blue potion
bottles**

**10 shooting
stars**

1 green potion bottle

2 red magnets

3 flaming burners

4 starbursts

5 mixing spoons

Magic potion

The fairies are using a secret recipe to make a magic potion.
Find all these things in the busy Potions Room.

Can you find?

6 purple potion bottles

7 pink brooms

8 purple flowers

9 bags of ingredients

10 blue potion bottles

**1 full
moon**

It's the witch!

The wicked witch is flying tonight! Find all these
things hidden in the spooky night-time scene.

**2 round
windows**

**3 pink
stars**

**4 dark
clouds**

5 fireflies

Can you find?

6 singing
birds

7 wise
owls

8 little
lanterns

9 witches'
broomsticks

10 yellow
stars

1 unicorn statue

2 pairs of scissors

3 toadstools

4 fairies with yellow ribbons

5 fairies with bows

Sleeping dragon

The fairies are tying down the sleeping dragon, in case he causes trouble when he wakes up. Spot all these things, but be quiet!

Can you find?

6 heart-shaped trees

7 rolls of ribbon

8 yellow birds

9 pink flowers

10 purple pins

Splish, splash, splosh!

The fairies are tiny and the raindrops are big! How many of these things can you find in the damp garden scene?

Can you find?

1 bluebell plant

2 sheltering spiders

3 resting butterflies

4 best friend couples

5 fairies in hats

Can you find?

6 fairies holding leaves

7 bees

8 fairy umbrellas

9 smiling raindrops

10 purple bugs

Candy corner

The fairies love this corner of the wood, where the plants grow sugary treats! Can you find all of these?

Can you find?

1 purple heart sweet

2 blue spiral sweets

3 empty baskets

4 yellow square sweets

5 baskets of heart sweets

Can you find?

6 yummy circle sweets

7 patterned square sweets

8 pink spiral sweets

9 candy canes

10 purple jelly beans

Can you find?

1 silver
moon

2 red cars

3 purple
owls

4 decorated
trees

5 shop
signs

The tooth fairies

The tooth fairies are delivering gold coins to children who have lost a tooth. Spot all of these things in the snowy scene.

Can you find?

6 extra-sparkly stars

7 bare trees

8 fairies holding teeth

9 dropped teeth

10 gold coins

Design a treehouse

The fairies are designing a treehouse for a competition.
Find all these things in the creative scene.

Can you find?

1 ruler

2 pencil pots

3 fairies with ribbons

4 rubbers

5 green crayons

Can you find?

6 purple
ink pens

7 paintbrushes

8 pencils

9 gold stars

10 pink
sequins

Can you find?

1 sleeping kitten

2 pink houses

3 hiding children

4 yellow houses

5 swans

Fairy wishes

The fairies are granting wishes for good children. What can you spot around the pretty village?

Can you find?

6 cars

7 heart-shaped trees

8 fluffy clouds

9 blue birds

10 wishing fairies

**1 jar
of sweets**

**2 cups
of tea**

**3 trays of
body lotions**

**4 bunches
of grapes**

**5 teddy
bears**

The Fairy Queen's bedroom

The Fairy Queen is feeling poorly. Search and find these things in her bedroom full of fairies trying to cheer her up.

Can you find?

6 bunches of flowers

7 pink hearts

8 pretty parcels

9 books

10 get well cards

Tiny dancers

It's the final rehearsal before the dance show.
Can you find all these things in the theatre?

Can you find?

1 rucksack

2 purple bows

3 hanging lights

4 ballet pumps

5 heart-shaped trees

Can you find?

6 flower displays

7 red roses

8 pink hearts

9 special star effects

10 pink fairy ballerinas

Fairy quilt

The fairies are busy making a beautiful quilt.
Can you spot all these things in the sewing scene?

Can you find?

**1 pair
of scissors**

**2 heart
squares**

**3 flower
squares**

**4 star
squares**

**5 butterfly
squares**

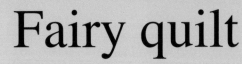

Can you find?

6 fairies like this

7 leaf shapes

8 yellow hearts

9 pink cotton reels

10 purple sequins

1 buzzy bee

2 blue horses

3 purple horses

4 pink horses

5 teddies

Fun at the fair!

The merry-go-round is lots of fun! How many of these things can you find at the fair?

6 butterflies

7 blue birds

8 daffodil plants

9 toadstools

10 toffee apples

1 blue bird

2 red butterflies

3 green butterflies

4 orange butterflies

5 purple butterflies

Butterfly day

It's the day of the annual butterfly race. How many of these things can you spot at the competition?

Can you find?

6 pink butterflies

7 blue butterflies

8 fluffy clouds

9 busy bees

10 pink flowers

Unicorn friends

Every evening, the fairies feed and groom the unicorns in the meadow. What can you spot in the happy scene?

1 jumping unicorn

2 little mice

3 fairies holding grass

4 buckets of apples

5 fairies with brooms

Can you find?

6 water buckets

7 unicorn shoes

8 sugar cubes

9 yellow birds

10 daisies

Midsummer's night

It's a magical moonlit night, and the fairies and unicorns are playing in the glade. Spot these things in the midsummer scene.

Can you find?

1 wicked witch

2 magic feathers

3 mystical flowers

4 midnight moths

5 fluffy clouds

Can you find?

6 magic wands

7 wise owls

8 glowing bugs

9 frolicking unicorns

10 tiny lanterns

Can you find?

1 bright moon

2 owls

3 lamps

4 dark clouds

5 strings of
bunting

Pretty castle

The fairies are decorating the castle so it twinkles in the darkness. How many of these things can you find?

Can you find?

6 purple fairy lights

7 waving fairies

8 lanterns

9 orange fairy lights

10 bright stars

Belles of the ball

It's the Fairy Queen's ball and the fairies are dressed for dancing. Can you find all of the pretty dresses in the fairy ballroom?

1 spotted ballgown

2 red ballgowns

3 white ballgowns

4 yellow ballgowns

5 blue ballgowns